The Traveller's Guide to the Solar System

Contents

*Written
by Giles Sparrow*

With your spacesuit checked, your suitcase packed and your boarding pass in your hand, you're ready to go!

Introduction

So you want to take a holiday across the **Solar System**? Great idea! It's an exciting place, and in the modern age of space tourism, lots of people are starting to look beyond Earth for an exotic holiday. You don't even have to go that far — there are hotels in **orbit** around Earth, and the **Moon** is just a short trip away. If you like, you can get your photograph taken next to the footprints of the first astronauts who landed on the Moon way back in 1969, and return the following **day**.

If you want to go to the Moon and beyond, you'll need a guidebook like this. We'll show you the highlights of **planets** and their moons ranging from nearby Venus to faraway Neptune, and take in some other interesting places along the way, including the icy comets and rocky asteroids that follow their own paths around the Sun.

So come with us and enjoy the best the Solar System has to offer. Play hopscotch in the rings of Saturn, go skiing on the Martian ice caps, or explore the mysteries of the Kuiper Belt. There's a lot to see and do — so let's get going!

The crescent Moon hangs over the launch complex.

Did you know?

Most planets behave as if they have a giant magnet inside them. This is usually the result of molten metal swirling around inside.

Getting around the Solar System

In order to reach the other worlds of the Solar System, you'll need to know a little about how things are arranged. The Sun is at the centre of everything, with eight major planets moving around it. The inner four – Mercury, Venus, Earth and Mars – are rocky and quite small. The outer four – Jupiter, Saturn, Uranus and Neptune – are much bigger and mostly made of gas and liquid. Most of the planets have their own moons – smaller worlds that go around them, just like our Moon. In-between and beyond these larger worlds, countless smaller chunks of rock and ice are also going around the Sun.

Every planet has its own orbit – the path it follows because of the pull from the Sun's **gravity**. Orbits don't have to be perfect circles; they can also be ellipses – stretched ovals that get closer to the Sun at one end than the other. The closer a planet is to the Sun, the faster it moves around its orbit and the shorter its **year**. Because of this, the positions of the planets are constantly changing, and every planet is a moving target. So you'll want to plan your trips around the time when your destination is at its closest to Earth.

A huge, traditional rocket, the Saturn V, took the first astronauts to the Moon.

Travel options

To get around the Solar System, you'll need some kind of spaceship. There are several types to choose from, but each has its good and bad points.

Traditional rockets use a controlled explosion from their fuel to push them forwards. They can get you up to a high speed, but the fuel is heavy, and the faster and further you want to go, the more fuel you'll have to carry.

Another way to travel is with an ion engine. This uses less fuel in a better way – instead of burning it, the engine uses electricity from solar energy to expel fuel particles, which pushes the spaceship in the other direction. Ion engines can run for a long time with a little fuel, but because they only push out a little fuel at a steady rate, you only speed up very slowly, and it can take months to reach high speeds.

Solar sails are another option – they are huge, reflecting sails that catch light and particles from the Sun and use it to push your spaceship forwards. They don't need any fuel, but they can only take you away from the Sun and, like an ion engine, they work very slowly.

Health and safety

Your spaceship will need to be heavily shielded to protect you from crashing into fragments of space dust during your voyage. Even a tiny impact can cause a lot of damage when you're travelling at high speeds. You'll also need protection from radiation, which is harmful energy from the Sun that is usually soaked up in Earth's **atmosphere** before it can reach us.

Once you're on your way, you'll probably spend most of the flight in zero gravity. It can take some getting used to, and a lot of first-time space travellers get ill. But even if you're not spacesick, you'll have some problems with weightlessness. Muscles get weak when they're not constantly supporting you against the pull of gravity, and eventually even your bones become brittle. The best remedy is to take lots of exercise every day.

Earth is the only planet in the Solar System with an atmosphere of air we can breathe, and a comfortable surface temperature.

Did you know?

It's a good idea to keep in shape with a treadmill on board. But don't forget to strap yourself down before exercising!

If you want to float in space or step onto the surface of another world, you'll need a good spacesuit. The suit acts like a portable spaceship, and provides you with life support for a few hours while you're exploring. Make sure you learn how to put it on properly, because any mistake could be fatal!

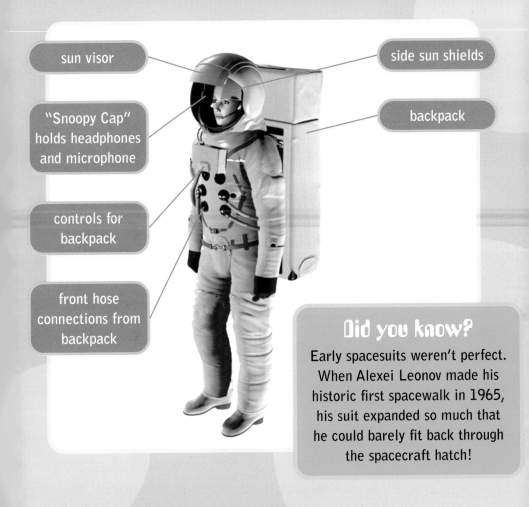

sun visor

side sun shields

"Snoopy Cap" holds headphones and microphone

backpack

controls for backpack

front hose connections from backpack

Did you know?

Early spacesuits weren't perfect. When Alexei Leonov made his historic first spacewalk in 1965, his suit expanded so much that he could barely fit back through the spacecraft hatch!

Within seconds of launch,
you're already above the clouds.

Lift off!

Getting off Earth is the hardest part of any space flight – our planet's gravity pulls everything towards it, and if you want to escape, you'll need to travel with high enough speed to overcome the pull of gravity and fly into the air and beyond. Because you'll soon be leaving Earth's atmosphere behind, wings won't be able to give you lift, so the usual solution is a rocket – a vehicle that uses the force created by exploding chemicals to push it into space (see "Travel options" on page 7).

Blasting off in a rocket is a rough ride – thrust from the engines will accelerate you rapidly, and you'll experience "G-forces" pushing you down into your seat, pulling your face backwards, and making you feel many times your usual weight. Your rocket will usually be designed in stages, each of which drops away once it has run out of fuel. Because of this, the spacecraft that reaches orbit around Earth is tiny compared to the rocket that launched it. It's only when the rocket stops accelerating, and you enter orbit, that the G-forces will suddenly disappear.

The view from orbit

Once in orbit, you'll hook up with a larger spacecraft that will take you out into the Solar System. Now is a good time to enjoy the view of Earth, and get used to weightlessness. Any spacecraft that's in orbit doesn't feel the effect of gravity because the inward pull of the Earth is perfectly balanced against the spacecraft's tendency to fly off into space. On board an orbiting spacecraft, you'll be able to float in weightless conditions, but be careful – anything you don't tie down will want to float off into space with the slightest nudge, even if it's just blown by the breeze from the air conditioning. Floating bits and pieces are a constant hazard in space, and you'll need to be especially careful with liquids, which form drifting blobs.

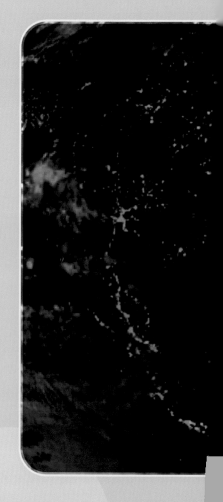

If you're feeling brave, you can take a spacewalk above the Earth in your spacesuit. The view over the night side is especially beautiful, with twinkling lights from Earth's cities appearing through the clouds. If you're lucky, you may even be able to see a meteor shower created by tiny dust particles – left-overs from the tail of a passing comet – burning up in Earth's atmosphere.

hanging in orbit over the night side of Earth

The Moon is a mix of bright cratered highlands and smooth dark seas.

A trip to the Moon

The Moon is Earth's only natural **satellite**, a ball of rock some 3,476 kilometres across. It orbits, on average, 400,000 kilometres away from Earth. That means it takes just a couple of days to get there, so it's the most popular destination for space tourism.

Unlike Earth, the Moon has no atmosphere, so you'll need to wear a bulky spacesuit on the surface. The suit won't bother you as much as on Earth, though, because the Moon's gravity is so much weaker – just one-sixth of Earth's. As you step out of your landing module and onto the Moon, you'll find you can make enormous leaps into the air and bounce along at high speed.

The lunar soil is a fine grey powder scattered with rocks. It's been pounded into tiny fragments by 4,000 million years of impacts from space. Larger impacts have formed craters – bowl-shaped dents gouged out of the Moon's surface. The near side of the Moon is divided into two types of terrain – smooth, dark grey "seas" with few craters, and brighter, rough, heavily cratered highlands.

Exploring the Moon

The Moon's number one tourist destination is the Sea of Tranquility – the spot where Neil Armstrong and Buzz Aldrin, the first men on the Moon, landed in July 1969. The so-called seas are actually huge, old craters that were flooded with molten lava by volcano eruptions about 3,900 million years ago. The lava wiped out traces of older craters across low-lying parts of the Moon, and then froze to form a smooth surface. Since that time, far fewer impacts have happened, so the seas have stayed quite smooth.

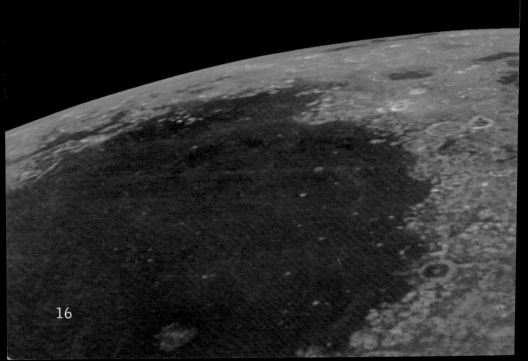

The Earth's gravity has slowed down the Moon's rotation so that it spins on its axis in just the same time it takes to orbit Earth. This means that one side of the Moon is stuck permanently facing Earth, while the "far side" is permanently hidden from view. Take a trip across it, and you'll see that it's almost entirely made of cratered highlands. The nearest thing it has to a sea is the crater Tsiolkovskii, named after a Russian rocket inventor. For some reason, the volcano eruptions that flooded craters on the Moon's near side never happened on the far side. This means that even the huge South-Pole Aitken Basin, the Solar System's largest crater – big enough to swallow western Europe – is hard to see from orbit.

speeding across the
Sea of Crises towards the
far side of the Moon

The nearest planet

Most of the time, Venus is the closest planet to Earth – it looks like a brilliant star from Earth, and never gets far away from the Sun in the sky. If you want to get there in a hurry, you'll have to wait for a period called "conjunction", when Venus and Earth line up on the same side of the Sun and are closest together, just 42 million kilometres from each other. Even then, Venus will still be 100 times further away than the Moon.

Venus is almost as large as Earth, and during the journey you should be able to see its distinctive shape through the flight deck windows. Around conjunction, most of the planet's sunlit side will be facing away from you, so you'll see a small crescent of brilliant creamy white.

From orbit, Venus's clouds are so bright that any detail is lost in the glare. The clouds completely hide the surface below, so you'll have to be ready for a bumpy, hair-raising descent if you want to see the real Venus. The planet might be beautiful from space, but on the surface it's the most hostile world in the Solar System.

Did you know?

Venus has a mysterious "ashen light", a faint glow across Venus's night side. Astronomers still don't know what causes it.

Venus's bright yellow clouds turn it into a brilliant crescent.

19

Earth's evil twin

Emerging from the clouds, you'll see that Venus's surface is covered in volcanic mountains, plains of solidified lava, and networks of fine cracks. Compared to the Moon, there are almost no craters from meteorite impacts – that's because they were all erased when massive volcanic eruptions flooded most of Venus's surface with lava, 500 million years ago.

Stepping onto the surface you'll have to be ready for anything, and wearing a spacesuit that's built like a suit of armour. The atmosphere on Venus is 100 times denser than on Earth, and that alone could crush you to a pulp.

Venusian volcanoes emerge through the clouds.

The air is mostly toxic carbon dioxide, clogged with sulphuric acid droplets and, at 470°C, the temperature is hotter than an oven. If anything goes wrong with your suit, you'll be dead before you know it!

Tourist hotspots on Venus include the towering volcanoes of the Eistla Regio region, surrounded by great lava plains. There are also web-like features called "arachnoids", and ring-like "coronae", all caused by lava bursting through Venus's surface in different ways. Despite all this, no one's yet seen an erupting volcano on Venus – maybe you'll be the first!

Did you know?

There is no water at all on Venus!

Mercury looks like a more cratered version of Earth's Moon.

Speedy Mercury

Mercury is a tiny planet at the hot end of the Solar System, orbiting the Sun in just 88 days. It's only a little larger than the Moon, and more heavily cratered, but it's still worth a visit, because it's a unique little world.

You'll have to catch it first, though. Because Mercury orbits closest of all planets to the Sun, it moves round its orbit much faster than the Earth. As you get closer to Mercury and start to see its surface features, you'll be able to tell that it's rotating very slowly – just once every 58 Earth days, or two-thirds of a Mercury year.

Mercury is covered in craters, but its biggest and most obvious feature is an enormous ringed impact basin some 1,300 kilometres across – the Caloris Basin. This is the scar left by a huge meteor impact billions of years ago, and it is surrounded by rings of mountains thrown up when shock waves tore through Mercury's crust – its outermost layer of rocks. The earthquakes spread all the way around the planet, and where they met up on the other side, they created a smashed-up landscape called "weird terrain".

Close to the Sun

Mercury is about as close to the Sun as you'd want to get — on the surface it's already hot enough to melt lead, and if you get any closer in, you'll need a heavily shielded spaceship. But you can get a good view of the Sun even from here — though you'll need to block out most of its light in order to see details. NEVER look at the Sun directly.

The Sun's outer surface might look smooth, but it's actually as rough as a stormy sea. The most obvious signs are the sunspots — dark areas that are much cooler than the surrounding hot surface. There are also towering pillars of flame called "spicules", and enormous loops called "prominences". Occasionally, the Sun belches out a huge cloud of hot gas called a solar flare.

All of this activity comes and goes over time, reaching a peak about every 11 years. This repeating pattern is called the "solar cycle", and its effects spread out across the Solar System, influencing the weather on Earth. The Sun's visible surface is topped by a hot outer atmosphere called the corona, which stretches for millions of kilometres into space.

Sunspots look dark against the brighter surface.

A prominence hangs over the edge of the Sun.

Riding a comet

One spectacular way to see the inner Solar System is to take a ride on a comet. Comets are lumps of ice that started life in the outer Solar System (see page 49), but get pushed onto paths that now bring them close to the Sun. A comet has an outer crust of dark chemicals that absorb heat from the Sun, warming up the hidden ice inside, until it starts to boil into water vapour. Jets of gas then burst up through the surface, and form a huge blob of gas called a "coma" around the comet's solid centre — the nucleus.

Time your visit right, and you'll be able to wander around on the comet's surface as it wakes up from its deep freeze.

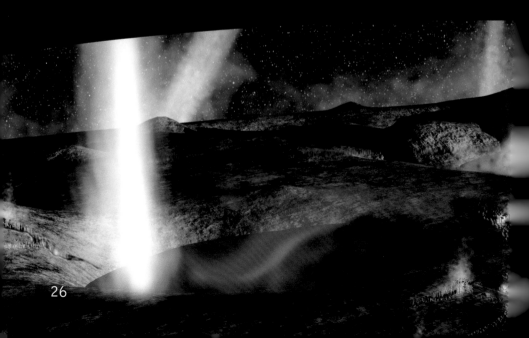

Then you can retreat to your spaceship and follow the comet as it swings round the Sun. As the comet runs into the solar wind of particles blowing out from the Sun, the gas and dust blowing off its surface are pushed away from the Sun, forming the comet's tail.

Comets suffer a lot of stress during their trips around the Sun, and they often break up completely. If they do survive, they may not return for thousands of years. A few comets come back in a much shorter time though, and the brightest and most famous of these is Halley's Comet, which comes back every 76 Earth years.

Jets of icy vapour shoot through cracks in the comet's surface.

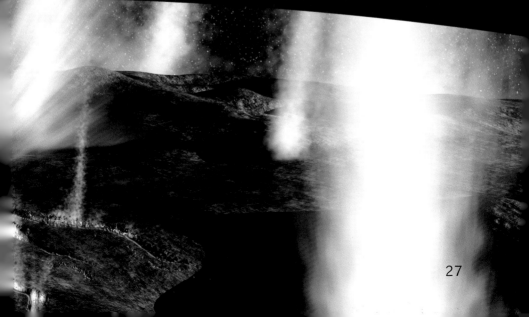

Mars's northern half is mostly smooth plains, but its southern half is cratered highlands.

Sightseeing on Mars

Mars is the Solar System's most popular tourist destination after the Moon. If you want to get there, you should time your trip for one of the close approaches to Earth which happen every two years or so.

The Red Planet, as it's often called, is a lot smaller than Earth or Venus, but bigger than the Moon or Mercury. As you enter orbit you'll be able to see that it has a thin atmosphere around it. The most spectacular sights from space are enormous volcanoes and a huge canyon called the Mariner Valleys, far bigger than Earth's own Grand Canyon.

If you land on Olympus Mons (Mount Olympus), you'll be standing on top of the biggest volcano in the Solar System. The only catch is that it's so huge you'll hardly notice it – 27 kilometres high and 500 kilometres across. If you want a really spectacular view for your holiday snaps, the best place for it is the enormous central crater.

The best way to see the Mariner Valleys is to take a low flight through them – standing on the edge of the plummeting ten-kilometre cliffs is not a good idea if you're scared of heights!

Red Planet mysteries

Many millions of years ago, Mars was a lot more like Earth. It still has ice caps on its north and south poles – they are well worth a visit, though when you get close to them, they're not much like the thick layers of frozen water on Earth. The Martian caps are mostly made of a gas called carbon dioxide, which makes up most of the planet's atmosphere, and creates bright frosts during winter. When summer comes to the north or south of the planet, most of the ice turns back into gas and the ice cap shrinks.

However, some of the Martian ice is made from water and this forms small permanent caps at each pole.

Frozen soil with ice just below the surface covers much of the northern hemisphere. In the past, Mars was warm enough for this ice to melt into water, and if you know where to look, you can see where it formed seas, carved out rivers, settled in lakes, and occasionally created enormous floods.

When Mars was warmer and wetter, there might even have been life here. It probably never evolved beyond bacteria, though, and certainly never produced plants, animals or intelligent life. But that hasn't stopped people being fascinated by the idea of life on Mars for centuries.

The Mariner Valleys are so big, you can only see them fully from orbit.

Did you know?

When spaceprobes first photographed Mars in detail in the 1970s, a lot of people thought they saw a mountain shaped like a human face. It turned out to be a trick of the light.

flying close to a double or "binary" asteroid

Did you know?

If you can find an asteroid, you get to name it. There's already asteroid 9007 James Bond, 17059 Elvis and 8748 Beatles!

Through the asteroids

Beyond Mars, there's a big gap in the Solar System before you reach the next planet, Jupiter. But this gap is not completely empty – it's filled with millions of small, rocky worlds called asteroids. Their orbits are kept in a rough ring around the Sun, called the Asteroid Belt, by the gravity of the larger planets.

The biggest and most interesting asteroids by far are Ceres and Vesta. Ceres is the largest asteroid, about 950 kilometres across. It's covered in craters, and like most asteroids its rocks have not changed much since the birth of the Solar System, 4,500 million years ago.

Vesta is very different from Ceres and most of the other asteroids. It has a bright surface made of frozen lava from volcanic eruptions, and a huge hole near its south pole – the scar from an enormous meteorite impact. Some astronomers think that Vesta is a chunk of a much larger asteroid that broke apart early in its history.

Most other asteroids are far smaller than Ceres and Vesta – just a few kilometres across. They are so tiny that they don't have the gravity to pull themselves into a sphere, so they are simply shapeless lumps of rock.

Jupiter's enormous Great Red Spot could swallow Earth twice over.

Giant Jupiter

Beyond the asteroid belt, the planets are very different. Instead of rocky worlds with atmospheres, they are enormous balls of gas and liquid. Jupiter is the nearest and biggest of these **gas giants**. It is the largest planet in the Solar System, more than 11 times the diameter of Earth.

As you approach Jupiter, the first thing you'll notice are its stripes – bands of cream, brown and blue cloud that stretch all the way around the planet. You'll soon be able to see oval storms swirling in-between the bands. Most of these are cream coloured, but the largest is usually red – it's called the Great Red Spot, and has been raging on Jupiter since at least the 1660s.

Jupiter doesn't have a solid surface to land on, but you can take your spacecraft on a dip into the clouds. You'll notice that different coloured clouds are at different heights in the atmosphere – blue clouds are the deepest, then brown and cream, with the red spots towering above their surroundings. The clouds stretch out into bands around the planet because of Jupiter's rapid rotation – despite its size, Jupiter spins once every ten hours.

Fire and ice

When you take a trip to Jupiter, you also get to see the most amazing system of moons in the Solar System. More than 60 moons of various sizes orbit the giant planet. Most of them are tiny captured asteroids orbiting millions of miles from Jupiter, but four are larger than Earth's Moon, and each very different from the others. In order of their distance from Jupiter, these are Io, Europa, Ganymede (the Solar System's largest moon) and Callisto.

Io is a volcano moon – heated up and twisted by Jupiter's gravity, hot sulphur bursts in fountains from below the surface, or bubbles away in craters.

Sulphur lakes bubble on the surface of Io.

Io is the most volcanically active world in the Solar System, and eruptions re-shape its surface every few decades.
As different forms of sulphur are laid down on the surface, they form brightly coloured splashes that make Io look like a burnt pizza from orbit.

At first, Europa seems like a quiet moon, covered in a thick layer of ice stained pink and blue by various chemicals.
But Europa has a big secret – underneath kilometres of ice there's a deep ocean of liquid water, where some people think there could even be life. The water is kept warm because Europa, like Io, is heated by Jupiter's gravity, producing undersea volcanoes that melt the ice.

Europa is covered with criss-cross tracks.

Frozen moons

Compared to Io and Europa, Jupiter's other pair of major moons are bigger, but less active – this is because they are much further from the giant planet and so do not get heated by its gravity.

Ganymede is a moon of browns, greys and whites, made from a mix of rock and ice. Counting the number of craters on different parts of the surface can tell you how old they are (because older areas have had more time to be hit by meteorites from space). You should be able to tell that the darker brown and grey areas are much older than the fresh white patches.

This chain of craters formed when a broken-up comet hit Ganymede.

Astronomers think that heat from Jupiter once warmed Ganymede so the old surface broke apart, and fresh, runny ice welled up from inside to form the moon's brighter patches, before the whole moon froze once again.

Callisto is different again. Its dark surface is pitted with countless craters, which have revealed sparkling bright ice from underground. Callisto never melted or had any volcanic activity, so its surface has preserved every impact scar from its long history.

Close up, Callisto looks like a disco glitterball.

Approaching Saturn, you start to see detail in its countless rings.

Ringworld

Saturn, the sixth planet from the Sun, is best known for its enormous system of rings. All four giant planets have rings, but Saturn's are the most beautiful by far. As you get closer to the planet, you'll soon be able to spot two broad, dark gaps in the rings. Depending on what angle you approach from, you might also see stripes where the rings cast shadows back onto the planet.

Saturn is the second biggest planet, and looks like a cream-coloured version of Jupiter. It has the same kind of storms and chemical layers inside it, but the colours are muted by a thin layer of white haze that covers the planet.

The rings stretch to more than three times the width of Saturn itself. As you enter orbit, you'll be able to see that each of the broad, flat rings is actually made up of countless narrow "ringlets". Each ringlet in turn is made up of millions of chunks of ice, ranging from small pebbles to boulders the size of houses – don't try to fly through them or your trip could end in disaster! The rings are probably the broken-up remains of a large comet or small moon, destroyed in a collision many millions of years ago.

Saturn's moons

Saturn, like Jupiter, has an enormous system of moons.
Only one is as big as the giant moons of Jupiter, but there are
a lot more medium-sized moons. One of the most interesting
is Enceladus, close to Saturn and covered in brilliant white
frosts. Another is Iapetus, which is much further out and has
a surface half-covered in dark, sooty dust. In the middle
of all these moons is Titan. It's easy to tell from the other
moons because of its size (almost as big as Ganymede),
and its thick orange atmosphere.

Saturn hangs above the
orange atmosphere of Titan.

Titan is the only moon in the Solar System with such a thick atmosphere, but it can be frustrating, because methane gas creates an orange haze that will block out your view of the surface.

To see what Titan really looks like, you'll need to take a trip through the clouds and down to the surface. Titan's landscape is quite a surprise, because it looks so much like Earth's – there are smooth, rounded hills, riverbeds, lakes and shallow seas. But as you'll soon find out, Titan's far too cold to have water in its lakes. Instead of water, Titan's rivers, lakes, snow and ice are made of methane. Temperatures here are so cold that this chemical can exist like water does on Earth, in ice, liquid and vapour forms. As the methane rivers carry methane rainfall from high ground back into the seas, they wear away the land around them, creating Titan's smooth landscapes.

Did you know?

Herschel, the astronomer who discovered Uranus, named the planet "George's star" after King George III. This earned him the job as the king's personal astronomer. The planet was later renamed.

Like the planet itself, the rings of Uranus are tipped on their side.

A world on its side

Uranus is twice as far from the Sun as Saturn, and quite a bit smaller, which makes it very hard to see from Earth. A trip will take several years, even with the fastest spaceship.

As you get closer, you should be able to spot five bright moons orbiting Uranus. In order from the planet, they are Miranda, Ariel, Umbriel, Titania and Oberon. But instead of circling the middle of the planet, they loop above and below it. This is a big clue that something strange is going on and, once you get close enough to see them, the planet's narrow rings will reveal its secret — Uranus is tipped on its side compared to all the other planets. It was probably knocked sideways by a huge collision early in its history.

This gives Uranus a very strange calendar. As the planet orbits the Sun every 84 years, each pole gets to see the Sun for 42 years, before being plunged into an equally long, cold night. The strange climate on Uranus stirs up its clouds so much that, during most of its long orbit round the Sun, it cannot develop any weather, and is an almost featureless blue-green ball.

The last planet

Neptune is the outermost of the major planets – roughly the same size as Uranus, but slightly bluer in colour. As it looms out of the darkness, you'll soon notice that it's quite different from Uranus, with obvious weather, including huge dark storms and fast-moving white clouds. In fact, Neptune has some of the fastest winds in the Solar System, with speeds of 2,100 kilometres per hour.

A dark storm comes into view as Neptune looms from the darkness.

Neptune's system of moons is very different from those around the other giant planets. It has just one large moon, called Triton, and it goes the "wrong way" around the planet. Astronomers think that Triton started life in the Kuiper Belt (see page 49), and was then caught up in Neptune's gravity. As it fell into its new orbit, Triton's own gravity played havoc with Neptune's original moons, so that today only a handful of the smaller ones survive.

Triton itself is well worth a visit. As you fly in, you'll see that it has two distinct types of landscape – bubbly blue "cantaloupe terrain" and flatter, greyish brown areas with dark streaks across them. If you land close to the dark streaks, you'll discover their secret – they're actually plumes of gas and dust that erupt from the surface like Earth's geysers. Triton should be a deep-frozen world, but the heat generated by Neptune's gravity helps to warm it up and keep it active.

Triton's streaky surface

flying towards Pluto
and Charon

The frozen wastes

Out beyond Neptune, you're entering the Solar System's frozen outer limits. By now, you're so far from the Sun that it just looks like a bright star.

Beginning around Neptune's orbit is a doughnut-shaped ring of **icy worlds** called the Kuiper Belt. Some of these icy worlds are deep-frozen comets on the outer edges of their orbits, but others are larger. The most famous of these, Pluto, was counted as a planet up until 2006, but when astronomers found a new world called Eris that was larger than Pluto, they decided that all the large residents of the Kuiper Belt should be called "dwarf planets" to keep them separate from the larger inner planets.

Pluto is still well worth a visit if you're out this way. It has three moons – the largest, Charon, is more than half the size of Pluto itself.

Way past the Kuiper Belt, a shell of deep-frozen comets, called the Oort Cloud, surrounds the entire Solar System. We know it's there because its comets sometimes fall towards the Sun, but it's far beyond the range of any spaceship, and almost half way to the nearest star.

How the Solar System formed

The Eagle Nebula is a cloud where stars are forming today.

Solar System history

The Sun, together with all the planets, moons, asteroids and comets that orbit it, formed from a huge cloud of gas and dust called a nebula, about 4,550 million years ago. Astronomers think that the gravity of a passing star, or the blast of a nearby supernova (an exploding giant star) pulled or pushed the cloud together. As it got denser, it began to collapse under its own weight.

Different parts of the nebula were moving in different directions, but as it collapsed, they evened out until the cloud was spinning one way. As more material fell into the centre, the cloud spun faster and faster. It also started to flatten out into a disc.

As the centre of the disc got denser, it also got hotter – hot enough to glow. Eventually, it grew into our Sun.

Meanwhile, smaller clumps of gas and dust in the disc around the Sun were also collapsing under their own weight, forming "protoplanets". Close to the Sun, there was less gas and the protoplanets came together to form today's **rocky planets**. Further out, there was more gas, which collapsed in huge clumps to form the giant planets.

Glossary – do you speak astro?

atmosphere   a shell of gas held around a planet by the pull of its gravity

day   the time a planet takes to rotate once

gas giants   the four outer planets of the Solar System, made of small rocky cores surrounded by a deep layer of gas

gravity   a force created by objects with a large amount of material (such as planets), which pulls other objects towards them

icy worlds   moons or small outer worlds that have a large amount of ice mixed with their rock – the ice being any frozen chemical, not just water

moon   a natural satellite of a planet, that may have formed in orbit around the planet, or been captured later by its gravity – the Moon (with a capital "M") being Earth's own satellite

orbit   the path any moving object takes around another one because of the effect of gravity

planets   large balls of rock or gas that orbit the Sun and have swept the region around their orbits clear of other material

rocky planets   any of the four planets of the inner Solar System that are made from solid rocks

satellite   any object that orbits another one because of gravity, like moons, which are natural satellites, and all the human-made satellites now scattered across the Solar System

Solar System   the Sun and everything in orbit around it

year   the time a planet takes to make one orbit around the Sun

Index

Solar System must-sees

The Moon is an airless ball of rock, but since it orbits Earth, it's a popular destination for a short break.

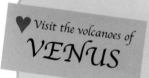

Venus is the same size as Earth, but has a choking atmosphere and is covered in volcanoes.

Mercury is the smallest planet, the closest to the Sun, and the fastest moving.

The Sun is at the centre of the Solar System – an enormous ball of exploding gas that holds everything together through its gravity.

Mars is the planet most like Earth, with lots of interesting things to see. It was probably even more like Earth in its past.

Jupiter is the first and largest of the gas giant planets. It has four large moons, including volcanic Io and ice-covered Europa.

Saturn's main attraction is its system of rings. Its largest moon, Titan, has a thick atmosphere, and a surface that looks surprisingly like Earth's.

Uranus was knocked onto its side early in its history, and has the strangest seasons of any planet.

Stormy Neptune is the last planet. Its largest moon, Triton, is a captured world from the Kuiper Belt.

 Ideas for reading

Written by Clare Dowdall BA(Ed), MA(Ed)
Lecturer and Primary Literacy Consultant

Learning objectives: make notes on and use evidence from across a text to explain events or ideas; reflect on reading habits and preferences and plan personal reading goals; plan and manage a group task over time using different levels of planning

Curriculum links: Science: Earth, Sun, and Moon

Interest words: asteroids, atmosphere, gravity, meteorite, orbit, protoplanets, satellite, Solar System, supernova

Resources: other text books about the Solar System, 3D model of the Solar System, ICT

Getting started

This book can be read over two or more guided reading sessions.

- Ask children in pairs to note ten things that they know about the Solar System.

- Share these ideas and decide whether they are true or false. Raise and list new questions based on them.

- Name all the planets known in the Solar System, using a visual resource. Explain that the text will provide information about visiting each planet and other phenomena.

- Read the cover and the blurb together. Discuss what it might be like to holiday in outer space and what preparations would be needed.

Reading and responding

- Look at the contents together. Decide how the group can organise their reading to answer the questions raised earlier (in pairs, sharing the task, etc.).

- Model how to answer a question by using retrieval devices (contents/index) and skimming and scanning to locate information.